Early years on a shoestring

Enabling environments on a budget

Hope you Bag a Bargain!
Kirstine

by Kirstine Beeley

Cover design by Stephanie Breen
Book design by Design Dejour www.design-dejour.co.uk

Published by Playing to Learn - Kirstine Beeley www.playingtolearnuk.com

ISBN 978-0-9955315-3-6

Photography courtesy of Treehouse Preschool, Winslow, Buckingham Park CE School, Aylesbury, Drayton Preschool, Love 2 Learn Nursery - The Curiosity Approach, Anna Lucas - Lucas Training & Consultancy Ltd

Printed in Great Britain

Although every precaution has been taken in the preparation of this book, the publisher and author assume no responsibility for errors or omissions. Neither is any liability assumed for damages resulting from the use of information contained herein.

With thanks to Louise Wetherall and Sarah Kingham for their patience in helping to edit the book and to all the staff and children at Treehouse Pre-School, without whom this book would not have been possible.

Contents

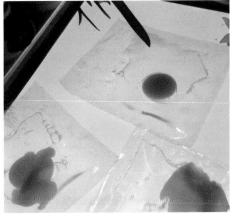

Introduction

One of the things which has become blatantly obvious over the past few years is the amount of practitioners that are fighting to provide high quality early years provision on increasingly tighter and tighter budgets. This coupled with a move away from brightly coloured, plastic heavy, settings to those which are softer, more homely and embrace natural materials has led to an upsurge in the use of upcycled, recycled and repurposed resources. As a teacher practitioner in a charitable preschool myself and working closely with thousands of childminders over the years, I have had to look at how we can maximise our learning potential whilst spending as little as possible. Over the past 11 years as an early years training consultant I have built a reputation for offering training based on these treasures and budget finds. With private day care and maintained schools and nurseries now under the same financial restraints I wanted to produce a resource to help ease some of the strain. Jokingly referred to as the "pound shop queen", I thought it was about time I shared some of my secrets about how to make best use of your money without compromising on learning quality. Although this book looks to the English EYFS framework (DfE 2015) as its basis, the ideas within should be easily transferable to other early years frameworks and ways of working. As well as offering specific ideas about resources you can use with young children, I hope to also show you some of the ways you can source cheap and often free materials for your settings. With a little bit of planning and quite a lot of brass neck it is amazing what you can find, and ultimately if you don't ask you won't get! What's the worst they can say... NO?!?!

As readers of my other books will already know, I am a huge advocate of child led learning environments and believe that best practice in early years lies away from structured, pre-planned activities. Although the book is based around the main areas of learning and development within the EYFS, it is important to remember that in resourcing an exciting, inviting and engaging environment in early years, learning does not happen in neat little subject labelled boxes. Learning is intertwined with other areas and accessed via the Characteristics of Effective Learning. A competent early years practitioner will look for the learning within child led play and draw out the opportunities to support and scaffold development across all areas. The book therefore only offers suggestions of ways to maximise potential for learning in specific areas and NOT definitive activities. Where any one child will take a specific resource is anyone's guess. This book looks to help you source loads of different open ended materials and aims to show some of the ways that children may choose to use them.

I also wholeheartedly believe that best practice comes from sharing best practice and therefore I would like to thank all the amazing early years people across the world who have inspired me with ideas for resources. We all need to make sure that we are constantly learning and striving to improve and modify our provision, if we are to ensure the highest possible learning potential is maintained. No setting is perfect. The children and staff in it will be ever changing and new lines of inquiry and exploration will open up everyday. Learn to go with the flow and enjoy the amazing ride that is being an early years practitioner!

Kirstine ☺

Personal, Social and Emotional Development

It's worth remembering that Personal, Social and Emotional Development (PSED) alongside Communication and Language, and Physical Development are identified as prime areas within the EYFS for a reason. Without their development, access to more specific areas of learning just isn't possible. Children need the physical skills to be able to write, to move, to hold tools and to manipulate equipment. They need to be able to express their ideas and needs across the whole curriculum and in life generally; and probably most importantly of all, in order to do any of these things, they need to build confidence in their own abilities, to feel able to express and explore their own ideas and to have faith in their voices being heard and supported by sensitive adults around them. Within the EYFS our primary focus needs to be on building these lifelong learning skills which will serve them well both now and in the future.

Confidence and independence

Building confidence and independence in young children is NOT about sitting them in a circle and following a carefully planned adult led activity. It is about looking at your environment and thinking "how can I enable this so that children feel confident, independent, supported and valued?". We, as practitioners need to reassess our surroundings and routines and ask ourselves if there are things that we are doing for the children that they could, given support and encouragement, do for themselves. Can they serve their own snack? Pour their own water? Wash up after snack? Put their own clothes on when changing? Or select their own paint or playdough? All of these things are simple to change, cost little or nothing to implement and have potential to build every child's sense of achievement, confidence and self-worth as well as developing their independent learning skills.

Independent access

When faced with a limited budget the process of enabling your environment so that children can access resources and activities independently is actually a blessing. There really isn't a need for expensive pieces of 'educational' furniture from the latest catalogue, however lovely they may look. The key to an enabling environment in early years is to view the setting or area in terms of skills rather than finished tasks and therefore when building independence, it does not matter what the resources are stored in or on as long as they are assessible to the children and easily moved to where the children choose to play and learn. As most children under five years, and a lot over, choose to work on the floor or at low level there often ceases to be a need for large pieces of plastic drawer filled furniture at all. Ask yourself, "can my children find what they need?" and "if they choose a resource to play with, can they transport it to the area where they are most likely to be able to use it and feel actively engaged with it?".

The addition of baskets and bags, easily and inexpensively sourced from charity shops and car boot sales, gives children the ability to choose and to move. Adding cable reels or wooden fruit crates can offer basket storage at child level for only a fraction of the price of a drawer unit and leaves money to be spent on other, more directly engaging resources. At this point I probably need to point out that the traditional view of everything in its place and carefully labelled with a nice computer-generated laminate is not in keeping with trying to promote independence. Just because it has a label on it does NOT by a process of osmosis lead to children reading! Children generally struggle to lift and move a tray packed full of plastic toys, often resulting in a big pile on the floor and an irate teacher! Taking just a few resources and putting them into a small basket not only helps children to see and self-select but if said basket is not dripping with laminated text then the need to put absolutely everything back in the right place is also removed. Leaving practitioners, and children, free from long "tidy up times" and allowing staff more time to play with and alongside the children and to ultimately support more learning. When helping children to make informed choices and develop independence less is definitely more!

reuse ... recycle ... reclaim

Home from home

One of the most important things we in early years are tasked with, is ensuring children feel safe, happy and at ease in our settings. It is our job to ensure that children's transition from home to us is as smooth as possible. We also must accept that a lot of what children learn in the world happens outside of their time with us and hence it is really important that we are aware of what their home settings are like and we try and make our own as much of a home from home as we possibly can. There is much that we can do to our environments to ensure that they feel comfortable, welcoming, safe and offer all the curious opportunities that a real home would.

By softening clinical settings with home furnishings and 'home' furniture we immediately make our settings more welcoming and inviting for children. Adding curtains, blinds, cushions, plants and pictures all help to add to the homely feel. You can soften harsh industrial lighting by draping fire proofed fabric from ceilings and walls.

It is widely accepted that children learn best by replicating what they are familiar with and hence by adding 'real' items to our setting we can invite them to revisit familiar situations. Real teapots, cups and saucers offer lots of opportunity for talk and role play alongside huge opportunities for maths talk and science exploration if we add fruit teabags or herbs to our offering. Try adding lamps, ornaments, battery powered candles and flowers for even more homely touches and talking points.

The lovely thing about using 'real' items when you are on a tight budget is that they are easy to source from charity shops, car boot sales, jumble sales and often found free at the back of cupboards or sheds. In using them in our settings we are giving our forgotten treasures a new and exciting lease of life.

One of the key things I always recommend any setting, school or otherwise, is to get hold of a sofa. I don't mean an expensive child sized sofa from an overpriced resource catalogue. I mean a REAL soft, snuggly sofa with room for an adult and a couple of children at least! Why? Well I will revisit the issue again in the literacy section, but in its simplest form, we are here to build relationships with adults in our settings, to develop a bond of trust and nothing does that better than the opportunity to snuggle up on a sofa and share a book, a story or a rhyme. We must remember that our children, even those at school, are still VERY young and attachment and interaction with adults is essential for building confidence and a sense of wellbeing and safety. We cannot do this if we are always sat on a chair above the children or stood towering over them as we talk at them. Sofas also offer a relaxed place where children are able to talk openly with peers and adults and of course a sofa immediately makes your setting look more like home and less scary and establishment like. The additional benefits of a sofa are made clearer in the literacy section of the book.

Second-hand sofas can be sourced via freecycling pages on the internet, through charitable furniture warehouses or just by putting out a plea to family and friends. Just make sure your sofa has the relevant fire safety labels (charity furniture shops must have these to be able to sell them).

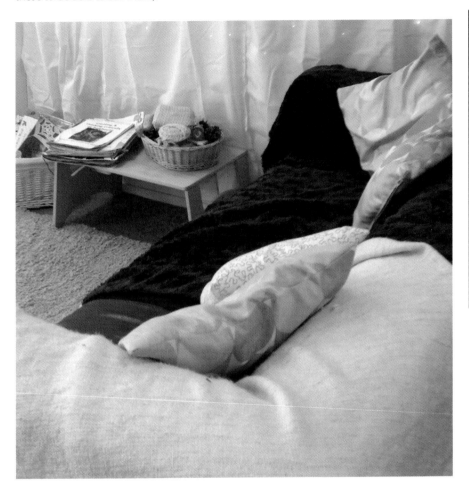

Real items and safety

I am often asked about the safety of using real items in early years and my view is that as long as they are risk assessed and supervised their learning potential far outweighs any concern about possible breakage. After all children could fall and land on a pencil or trip and break a plastic sand timer but we don't remove them from our settings! It is all about the careful balance of risk against benefit. If the benefits to learning outweigh the risk then it's worth having a go at least.

Reflecting children's own lives

As well as reflecting the environments in which our children live and feel comfortable, we also need to reflect their experiences at home. Giving children as many links to home as possible will help to make our settings seem less of a scary, separate place and feel more like a smooth addition to what they already know.

One easy and really cheap way of bringing the home into our settings is to get families to put together a family photo book. A selection of photos of family members, pets, favourite toys etc. in a cheap album offers a great talking point to help adults build relationships with the children and also a safe option to revisit when a child is having an emotional wobble or is in need of a little reassurance.

Photo albums can be purchased really cheaply from supermarkets, pound shops and online and the small amount of expense (often much less than £1 each) is far outweighed by the emotional and social benefits. Making these books available to children at all times means they are always there for them to revisit and to talk about with friends and staff (a great introduction to using books carefully and correctly too!).

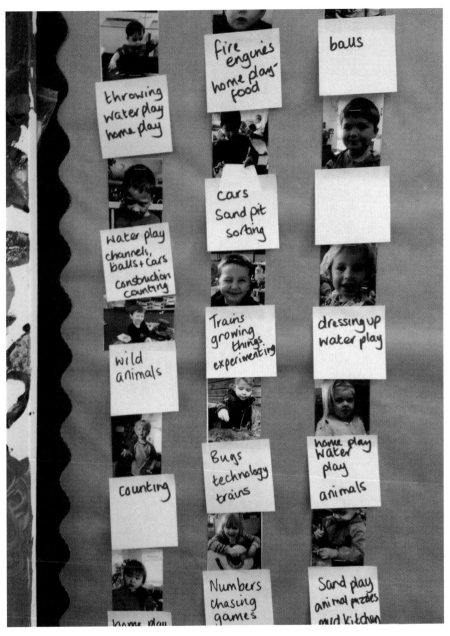

Having a "what I like wall" can help you to know what makes children tick outside of the setting and can guide how you enhance your resources. It also acts as a great link with parents and lets them feel part of the ongoing development process.

Staff have homes too!

It always makes me chuckle when children ask if I live at the setting or if I used to sleep in my desk drawer in the classroom! I think it is really important that in softening the setting to make it more welcoming for children that we also look at how we portray ourselves. Are we regimented humans who always wear uniform and focus only on learning and outcomes? Or are we humans with families, interests, pets and flaws of our own? One great, and cheap way of portraying the latter is to swap your corporate staff pictures on your parent noticeboards/entrance halls for framed pictures of staff either with their own families or pets or just enjoying doing something which is special to them. Using a wide range of interesting frames from car boots or charity shops adds to the interest and offers quirky, human feel to your parents' first contact with you.

reuse ... recycle ... reclaim

Not about bikes and trikes

One thing we are often guilty of in early years is thinking that just because we have done something a certain way for 30 years it is still the right way to do it. What this leads to is settings that look similar, if not exactly the same, as they did decades ago rather than settings where every element of the provision has been thought out and added to with learning potential in mind.

Physical development provision must be a prime example of this. Many settings still have outdoor spaces full of bikes, trikes and scooters and many reception classes still break to get children dressed for P.E. sessions and troop them off to the hall for a well-planned scheme of exercise and movement.

I must point out at this point that nowhere in the EYFS does it say that we should teach children to ride a bike or a trike! In fact, the skills outlined in physical development in early years are so far removed from bikes and trikes that their very inclusion can justifiably be questioned.

As with other areas of learning and development we have to ask ourselves, "what are we looking to achieve?". In early years, we are looking to provide children with the skills they will need to help them access on-going learning in the future both inside and outside of our settings. With bikes and trikes, the learning potential, to me, seems hugely limited. Apart from learning that only one child can use it at a time and building your frustration, alongside the obvious need to wear closed toed shoes as an adult, there seems little other benefit; even if we do laminate the bikes and car parking spaces to within an inch of our lives!

Children need to learn to build gross motor skills (large movements of limbs and body which lead to increased strength and co-ordination in arms, legs and general body control) alongside fine motor skills (building smaller, more controlled, movements of fingers, hands, feet and toes). The development of both sets of skills allows children to be able to negotiate their environment safely without tripping or falling, to be able to climb steps and stairs and to be able to manipulate tools, clothing, food and objects with greater confidence and precision.

With this skill set in mind it is important that we enable our environments with resources that actively promote the possibility of learning in this area. We have to build in opportunities to move over, under and through differing levels and to explore a wide range of materials with both large limb and fine finger movements. Looking at it like this actually frees you up to create some amazing, engaging and inviting environments without the need to spend a fortune on specialist equipment.

Gross motor & reclaiming materials

Some of the best ways I have found to offer the chance to build gross motor and balancing skills in early years are by adding a variety of open ended materials, many of which can be reclaimed for free from local suppliers.

Adding tyres of all sorts to your environment offers lots of chances to step up, in and over; to roll, to lift and to slide with muscles in backs, shoulders and upper arms. Adding gravel to tyres and stacking can give easy and cheap steps for children to learn to negotiate as they get used to what their bodies can and cannot do and grow in confidence at their own skills.

Adding cable reels of different sizes can give the chance to roll, lift, climb and build using a resource that is both weather durable and costs little or nothing. Cable reels can often be sourced by contacting a local electrical supplies company. Try an online business directory and hit the phones! Many businesses must pay to have these by-products of their industry removed and are glad for you to arrange to take them away. Make sure you choose reels that are free from splinters and sharp edges. Adding reels of different sizes and weights increases the possibility for open ended play and as a result the possibility of gross motor development.

One thing you can add to your outdoor setting cheaply is a gravel pit. Different to sand or mud play, digging in gravel offers great opportunities to build vital muscles in arms and backs. Filling big buckets then throws up lots of chances for co-operative play and maths language exploration. Children very quickly learn the meaning of 'heavy'!

A simple frame for a gravel pit can be built from reclaimed wooden pallets or offcuts of decking boards. You can then often persuade local building or turf suppliers to donate a bag of gravel or two to help you fill it. Worst case scenario you can get split bags at discounted rates from DIY and building suppliers. Don't be afraid to ask before you pull out the pennies!

Big plastic buckets can be sourced from builders, decorators or even from food shops such as fish and chip shops (make sure they are well cleaned before use). Building a collection of these in your setting will encourage children to fill with stones, sand, water or mud and to build gross motor skills as they move, lift and transport them.

Adding a collection of milk crates, bread crates and plank offcuts will give children open access to resources that they can build with, walk along, climb in – all of which are physical skills. Milk crates are easily sourced from local dairies and milkmen. Bread crates are often available upon request from supermarkets and smaller stores. You could even try sweet talking your online shopping delivery driver to leave a few plastic crates next time they visit! Remember if you don't ask you will never get! Decking board offcuts can be sourced from local landscaping and building firms.

Drainpipes and guttering off cuts can be sourced from local roofing contractors and smaller plastic piping from local plumbers.

Some DIY stores also have schemes where offcuts and end of line materials can be made available to local schools, nurseries and other childcare providers. Ask in stores for details.

Use it up!

You don't always have to phone around or scour the local industrial estate to find cheap resources for physical development. There are often resources much closer to home which can open up a world of physical possibility. I visit lots of settings and scrap stores where there are heaps of old powder paint tubs lurking in the back of a store cupboard. Excess powder paint is great for using outdoors to build gross motor skills. Throw paint at the floor then offer children child sized mops, brushes and buckets of water to move and mix the colours. The same goes for shaving foam in puddles on a rainy day. If you don't have powder paint in your own cupboards try asking your local school or scrapstore. Their trash is often your treasure!

You don't have to spend a fortune on child sized mops and brushes either. Adult versions can often be purchased with wooden handles for a couple of pounds. Just saw off the handle to child height and sand off the end! In the back of the same storage cupboards or sheds you can often also find old decorating brushes which are great for mark making with water and at the same time build gross motor skills.

Try taping paint brushes to the end of bamboo garden canes to encourage increased gross motor development

Fine motor – kitchen cupboard resources

Fine motor development also has to be viewed as a skill set rather than a lot of activities with specific outcomes. In early years, we are aiming to build up both strength and co-ordination in wrists, hands and fingers so that children are more able to use tools, move objects, dress themselves, feed themselves and eventually pick up a pencil and mark make. With this is mind our environments need to be enriched with lots of possibilities which offer access to these skills on a daily basis.

The joy of fine motor development with young children is we probably have a lot of what we need in our kitchen cupboards, sheds or craft boxes! We must focus our efforts on stocking up on items that offer opportunities to squish, squeeze, pinch, twist, poke and scoop. Anything that builds muscles in our hands and fingers or develops hand-eye co-ordination.

Rice

A couple of kg bags of long grain rice will set you back less than a pound and can have endless possibilities. If you dye the rice and add in a wide variety of containers and scoops then the opportunities for learning are endless. Paper bags for filling can be sourced cheaply online or from a local greengrocer. Plastic shot glasses from pound stores make great scoops and you can recycle scoops from washing powder and washing whitener tubs or baby milk tins. Adding lots of spoons of different materials from charity shops or car boot sales adds multi-sensory exploration and loads of potential for maths and problem solving alongside the fine motor skills.

How to dye rice

Divide your dry long grain rice into a number of zip lock bags depending on how many colours you require. Add a blob of antibacterial hand gel to each bag (this not only acts as a transfer medium for colour but helps to keep nasty bugs at bay in the rice and deters children from eating the rice due to the taste!). Next add a tiny bit of food colouring gel. It is well worth investing in good quality food colouring gel from online suppliers as it goes a lot further and the colours are brighter. For really bright colours use neon food colour gel. Close the bag, ensuring air is squeezed out. Move the rice around until it is fully coloured. Open the bag and leave to dry for about an hour. The alcohol in the hand gel will evaporate and mean your rice is dry and ready to use really quickly. Then move on to the next bag and do the same with another colour.

Spaghetti

A really cheap resource which is great for threading beads or buttons onto or for cutting and snipping when cooked and coloured. Spaghetti offers lots of chances to explore maths language and problem solving as well as building co-ordination and hand strength.

How to colour spaghetti

Firstly, cook the spaghetti as you would do normally. A whole packet will give you enough for a number of colours. Drain and rinse the spaghetti with cold water to remove any excess starch. Divide the spaghetti into large bowls depending on how many colours you require. Fill the bowls with cold water. Add food colouring gel to each bowl and stir so water is fully coloured. Leave overnight ideally or at least for a few hours until spaghetti has absorbed the colour. Drain and rinse off excess colour. Place into a tray or scooped out pumpkin for exploration and fine motor fun.

Recycled treasure

I love the fact that in early years the things that most people throw away become amazing resources in our settings. From wooden curtain rings and mug stands to bracelets and kitchen roll holders and even washers and metal egg cups. There are lots of example of cheap or free resources which I have used over the years that all promote and extend fine motor development as well as offering huge potential for open ended learning in other areas.

reuse ... recycle ... reclaim

Playdough

Probably one of the cheapest, easiest and most powerful fine motor tools available to you in early years. Making your own playdough and offering it as part of a self-serve playdough bar gives lots of finger muscle-strength building on its own. If you then develop the tools you have on offer to enhance fine motor develop further the potential for learning is limited only by the children's imagination. Try adding small coloured matchsticks (you can colour your own by soaking overnight in coloured water and drying), or small shells, glass beads or buttons that require children to pinch. Always risk assess with small parts and be aware of children who mouth objects, but small parts don't have to be avoided altogether as they offer great learning potential. Adding fresh herbs or lavender and scissors to your playdough bar gives lots more chances to build scissor skills and hand strength while exploring the smells and textures involved (early science at its best and not a float or sink tank in sight!).

Quick and easy playdough recipe

Add the following to a bowl:

3 parts plain flour
1 ½ parts table salt
1 teaspoon of creme of tartar
1 tablespoon of vegetable oil
1 teaspoon of glycerine

Mix the dry ingredients with the oil

Add a few drops of food colouring gel to 3 parts of boiling water.

Add the water to the dry ingredients and stir until it comes together in a ball.

Empty out onto a flat surface and leave to cool for about 5 mins.

When cool enough to handle, knead the dough until you have a smooth dough and it is fully coloured. If too wet add more flour and if too dry add a few more drops of glycerine.

SAFETY NOTE – DO NOT USE BOILING WATER WITH CHILDREN AND ALWAYS WAIT UNTIL DOUGH IS COOL ENOUGH TO BE HANDLED.

Tinker station

One project I have really enjoyed recently is combining my reclaimed, recycled and repurposed materials to make a tinkering station. This has proven a real hit with children and is great not only for fine motor skills development but also for creativity and problem solving as well as open ended inquiry and questioning.

Look out for nuts and bolts which can be purchased in certain high street home stores as pick and mix bags for a very reasonable price. Or ask parents and grandparents to donate their odds and ends from their tool boxes.

Communication and Language Development

Your biggest asset in this area of development is free (well apart from the wage bill) and is you and your staff. We as practitioners have to be the key to initiating talk and building children's confidence to express their own ideas and findings. We need to make sure we listen carefully, give time for them to respond to our questions and offer lots of open ended opportunities to build on language. Remember a two year old can take up to 10 seconds to process a question before they are able to offer any kind of response! As well as having a caring, supportive and sensitive staffing team we can also enable our learning environment to maximise language potential.

If children are exposed to settings where they are only ever able to access activities which are narrow and adult led they will lack both the confidence to try and explore new things but also the ability to communicate their own needs and ideas. As discussed in the PSED section of the book, building our settings to support independent choice not only builds confidence but children's ability to express themselves. So, a communication friendly setting will offer lots of open ended and creative resources that give children the opportunity to take the learning in their own direction.

It will also contain lots of inspiring, exciting and unusual objects that children are actively encouraged to explore and engage with. It is these talk prompts that will engage children and get them talking and asking questions. So we should look at our settings and assess if we have things openly available that scream "come and look at me", "what am I?", and "what do I feel like?". Here, again, 'real' objects sourced from charity shops or car boot sales can be some of the most exciting and engaging. Building up a collection of objects that make us think "wow" is well worth the time and effort and allows us to rotate the resources on offer to the children. Having them readily available for exploration around the setting will encourage lots of excited discussion with peers and adults. Select your objects on the basis that they provoke inquisitiveness and curiosity which will in turn lead to discussions and questioning.

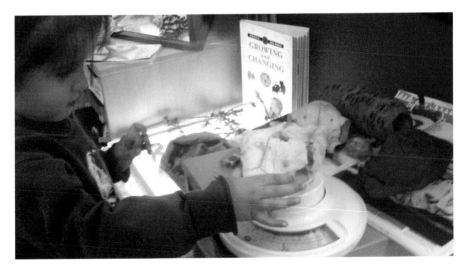

Talking spaces

Alongside your staff and your exciting resources, you can also develop spaces where children can get comfortable and relaxed and where they are likely to engage in talk with peers and adults. In early years, children really like crawling into small spaces where they feel safe and contained. These are the talk spaces where communication skills and language can flourish. You can of course spend a fortune in a catalogue and buy a readymade arch or talk pod but that wouldn't be in the spirit of this book! There are also some really simple ways you can develop talk spaces in your setting.

Try repurposing the table you have stopped using because you have opened up your floor space to child led exploration. A table draped with some old voile curtains and furnished with some second-hand cushions will attract lots of interest and can be used in any free space at minimal cost. Why not try upcycling a baby's travel cot? We turned ours on its side and made it look exciting and engaging with drapes and throws and added soft cushions to make it even more appealing. Even adults can crawl into this talk space with children!

Cheap rose arches can be purchased for under £10 and can be adapted with drapes and material to create lovely cosy talk spaces.

Talking spaces need also to be developed for outdoors. Even though young children are more likely to talk outdoors than indoors because the sound is not bouncing around the walls and ceilings, there still needs to be thought put into enabling the communication opportunities outdoors. We have, in the past, repurposed our shed to make it into a welcoming talk space complete with bench and books for sharing and have also built a talk den using leaves and sticks. One of our children's favourite spaces is the crate den, made from a recycled builders brick crate and a piece of camouflage netting purchased cheaply from an online auction site.

We are really lucky to have sourced a real rowing boat, free from an online recycling site, which is used by children to talk, tell stories, have adventures and to cosy up in and share books. It is a prime example of what is possible if you search around and have the courage to ask!

Online sourcing

In the UK some of the most useful online sites for searching out materials for upcycling and repurposing include Freecycle, Freegle and Gumtree. Ebay and other online auction sites are also well worth keeping an eye on. I have personally found that if there is something specific that we are looking for then getting

all of our parents to put out a plea on Facebook, Twitter and Instagram can work really well.

Talk prompts

One really cheap thing we can do in any setting is to print off intriguing and exciting pictures that prompt children to discuss what they are seeing. Some settings have a daily picture for discussion. Others have a few pictures in a clear cube as a centrepiece for talk at snack time. There is no need to purchase expensive sets of pictures. A quick internet search will quickly find lots of options and pinterest.com has lots of boards of talk prompts.

Talking sofas

Once again our sofa plays a huge part in communication and language development. A cosy sofa offers a safe, secure and inviting space for children to sit and talk with adults or with other children. Surrounding it with exciting and engaging 'real' objects will maximise the talk potential too.

Real life reading

It never ceases to amaze me how we go crashing into early reading with synthetic phonics and formal reading schemes and hope that if the wind doesn't change direction our children will magically start reading! If we take some time to break down what is going on as young children start to read, it has an impact on the kind of environments we should be offering in early years. As young children experience a text rich environment they start to realise that marks carry meaning and with even more exposure can even recognise some familiar texts. By this I do not mean that you should laminate a label onto everything in your room! The text rich environment of which I speak is generally outside of our setting. Even young children very quickly start to recognise text around them such as shop signs, TV logos and food trademarks. It is these texts that we need to be looking to replicate in our settings and which provide us with a 'text rich environment' without the need for expensive purchases or even too much laminating. Adding packet labels to a window, real packets and tins into our role play and even developing a logo alphabet all give children the chance to 'read' and develop their confidence to approach familiar and unfamiliar text. These simple, yet cost effective, enhancements can also be tailored to reflect additional languages. Working with parents of children with EAL (English as an Additional Language) it is possible to add in packets and labels with other languages which the children are familiar with at home and which will help them to engage in imaginative play and talk as part of their role play. It is also worth remembering that there are lots of familiar texts that children come across in their lives that are not fiction or non-fiction books. Children love to read comics, cookbooks, TV magazines and newspapers and as such these too should be in abundance in our settings.

reuse ... recycle ... reclaim

Reading home from home

As well as adding these familiar texts to our child led environments we should question how we offer the chance for children to become confident with exploring books and other texts. At home children often enjoy snuggling up with an adult to listen to a story, to join in with a familiar rhyme or to talk about the pictures in a book. All great early reading skills. Yet the time spent in a safe, comfortable environment is part of the enjoyment and is what draws children back time and again to want to share and reshare books and stories. Yet, in settings, we often bring children to a table to sit alongside an adult to read a book that sits flat on a table while the adult concentrates on the child's ability to decode the

text. Surely if we recreate the warm, supportive, home from home environment which encourages enthusiastic readers we stand a better chance of engaging children more in the process of exploring books rather than just going through the mechanics of reading? With this in mind, the addition of cosy spaces and a real sofa where adults and children alike can snuggle up and really share the stories is essential in early years.

Remember the main thing we really want to instil in our children is a love of books rather than just an ability to decode and regurgitate text. Resource your setting with a carefully selected selection of engaging books that will really make children want to pick them up and share them with you. If you ask parents or even local charity shops you can usually build a good range of both story and fact books to distribute in all areas around your setting. Reading doesn't just happen in 'the reading corner'!

Early phonics

That said there is a need to introduce some element of synthetic phonics as children become more confident with exploring books and other familiar texts. Being able to hear sounds within words and to be able to break them apart and rebuild them is another skill that children use when learning to read (alongside recognising the shape of some key words, taking prompts from the pictures in a book and using the context already read to predict what happens next).

In the first instance, early phonics is all about listening to and differentiation between sounds. Be they instrumental sounds, body sounds or environmental sounds, children's ability to eventually be able to pick out specific letter sounds depends on these essential listening skills. These are really easy to facilitate on a budget by making up collections and games with everyday objects that you take time to explore with the children. Or just to look out for opportunities to point out letter sounds within children's open-ended play. Remember to be sensitive to the play and not to go charging in with your own adult led agenda or the children will be off and away!

Cheap and easy letters can then be added to your ranges of open ended resources that allow children to explore letters and letter sounds only when they are ready and within the context that they choose.

*Hair gel –
rhyming slime*

*Coffee, cups
and cars –
alliteration*

Upcycling materials

As well as reading materials, access to writing implements and mark making materials also has to be provided in all areas around your setting and in ways that mean children can take them to their play rather than just being able to write at a 'writing table'. Developing lots of portable containers full of exciting materials, pens, papers, chalks, pads and card will make writing an enjoyable activity within the children's own play. Adding whiteboards and pens to mud kitchens gives options for menu and recipe writing, adding clipboards and pencils give a chance to write lists of things children have collected and lots of envelopes and cards will enthuse children to write letters and postcards to family and friends.

Resources for these kinds of sets can be cheaply sourced at scrap stores where materials that are usually a by-product of a company are recycled for use by establishments such as ours for a fraction of the shop bought new price. Scrap stores offer access to lots of different materials to mark make on including cards, envelopes, paper rolls and wood offcuts (see *Useful Information* for details of how to find your local scrapstore). Why not try painting old pieces of wood or logs with chalk to encourage mark making? Even large pebbles, shells and wooden spoons can be used as surfaces for writing on and for sharing story ideas.

Black board paint on tree slices

Literacy

Pound shop resourcing out of season

Pound shops and bargain shops are in abundance across most countries now and are invaluable when delivering early years on a budget. They offer affordable mark making resources such as chalks, pens and pencils as well as some creative ways to hold mark making materials. As with natural resources make sure you stock up when you see things which are useful as they may only be available for a short time and yet be useful in your setting for much longer. Don't forget to think creatively in these shops, things you can find in the pet section or the gardening section could make great resources for writing, reading or even maths and creativity. I always work on the basis that if it makes me go "wow!" it will hopefully do the same for the children.

Note : Resources from retail outlets are not designed or tested for multi-user use so make sure you look carefully at their construction and always risk assess before using with children.

reuse ... recycle ... reclaim

More than just numbers

One thing that needs to be highlighted with early maths is that only a very tiny part of it involves number, and an even smaller amount involves written numerals (which are not relevant until children are starting to read and differentiating between marks that carry meaning). What is important is to recognise that maths is integrated into lots of what we do in our everyday lives and it is this maths that we need to reflect in our learning environments so that children can access maths skills and understanding as they play. Maths does not happen just because you put in a late night with the laminator and have wallpapered your garden accordingly! Children engrossed in play will not stop to look up and acknowledge your creation, however pretty it may look. We need to be looking for the potential for maths learning within child led, open ended play.

Open ended resources

When looking for maths learning in early years we need to ensure access to a wide range of open ended resources which have no right or wrong way of using them. The upside to this kind of resource, above an expensive catalogue sourced resource, is that they are cheap, easy to find and often free.

Stock your indoor and outdoor provision with a selection of tin cans (edges filed down for safety), buckets of all sizes, tubing, wood slices, spoons (different shapes, sizes and lengths), flower pots, teapots and cups, scales, socks, sticks, leaves, or glass beads. The list is endless but focuses on resources that can be donated, sourced free, recycled or purchased cheaply from online suppliers.

The power of open ended resources is in the way that children choose to use them. Their imagination and creativity becomes key and they end up not only accessing maths skills but problem solving, co-operative play and many other learning skills at the same time.

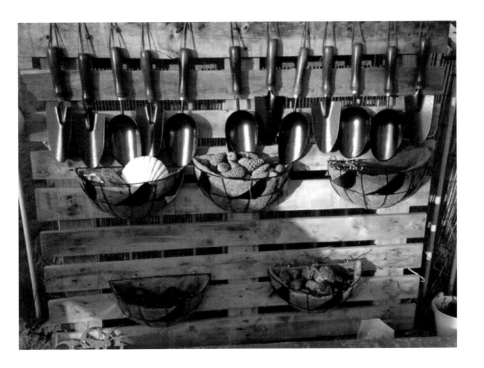

Nature's store cupboard

Counting is a much more complex skill than it may initially seem and actually does not involve written numerals until much, much later in the learning process. For children to fully understand that meaning of what 'two' or 'five' means they should experience counting objects in lots of different play scenarios. The first step in this learning process is to explore counting moveable objects and hence enabling our environment with loads of objects that can be moved as children say "one, two, three..." so that they learn that the last number name they say relates to how many they have.

When resourcing your environment with interesting, engaging and inviting objects with the potential for counting, one of the best places you can find free or at least very cheap resources is in nature's store cupboard. Collecting loads of natural objects, pine cones, acorns, leaves, sticks, shells, log slices etc. will provide not just interest but potential and possibility. Make sure that when you are out collecting you stock pile for the whole year so you don't run out when they are out of season.

Note: Collecting pebbles from shorelines and beaches is illegal in the UK due to its potential impact on coastal erosion so source your pebbles from garden centres and builders' merchants.

Mathematics

reuse ... recycle ... reclaim

Real life maths

Maths, like all other areas of early learning is best accessed with the child's own experience and understanding at its centre. We as practitioners need to look at our everyday lives and seek out the maths that occurs in our homes, in shops and out and about. We must then reflect these experiences as much as possible in our environments as these are children's first and most powerful experiences of maths with a purpose. Adding real tins to a home corner will give real experience of weight and size as well as 3D shapes, adding vegetables to your mud kitchen will offer opportunities for sharing, halving and exploration of size, weight and length. Mobile phones, TV remote controls, diaries, calendars, telephones, calculators and dummy credit cards give real experience of written numerals and lots of different containers of different sizes and shapes, from teapots to saucepans and dishes to spoons will give a multisensory opportunity to explore, size, volume, shape and measuring. These 'treasures to measure' bring so much open ended opportunity for maths learning that they are worth sourcing as a mathematical tool, in their own right.

Treasure to measure

Car boot sales, charity shops and the back of kitchen cupboards and sheds are your starting point for building your treasure stash. The use of containers that are made of different, non-plastic, materials is far from just an aesthetic choice. When children experience a new sensory sensation, they fire and rewire brain connections. The more sensory opportunities we offer them, the more connections they are building. We are building lifelong learning capacity as well as having a whole heap of play and learning fun!

A wide selection of pots, pans, cups, jugs, pots, containers and spoons in copper, brass, steel, silver and wood can open up so many engaging possibilities for play in water, sand or mud kitchens. Try to source selections of the same type of container in different sizes or different materials to give children the chance for open ended comparison and exploration.

With treasure to measure, someone else's trash will definitely be a child's treasure when it comes to offering potential for talking about and exploring capacity, weight, size, shape, more and less as part of imaginative play, problem solving and exploration of materials as potions, perfumes and pies are created.

Language of maths

As with other areas of learning in early years our staff are our best tool for scaffolding the language of maths. Looking for the learning as children play and modelling the mathematical words for what children are doing naturally rather than setting up closed, adult led activities where learning potential is limited and engagement negligible. You don't have to laminate loads of signs with maths words on to surround your water tray. Just make sure your staff are confident with the kinds of language they are expected to use and model. A small adult list to hand is useful or if you must have words have them up high where adults can make use of 'dead space' as a prompt.

Numerals

So, I can't really finish a section on maths development without talking about numerals but they are not last just by chance. Children must have a really good practical grasp of maths within a wide variety of situations before they even start to work with written numerals. The process of writing numbers is not really a mathematical skill as it is rooted in physical development, early mark making and writing skills. To resource your setting with numerals, try to make them real

and relevant. Add birthday cards, cake candles, remote controls, phones, etc. If you want to add more, just writing numbers on open ended resources such as pebbles, shells, flower pots etc will give an invitation to explore numerals without a narrow learning remit and allow children to explore them within other areas as they play rather than as a standalone skill. Remember maths is not a standalone subject, it is integrated into most play that children choose independently. We as the adults just need to be adept at looking for the learning and watching for sensitive 'teachable moments' within their play.

Positional language

As we have already seen in the *Physical Development* section of the book, the potential for cheap, upcycled and recycled resources that promote travel, balance and levels is huge. It is the children's use of these crates, planks, tyres, tunnels, etc. that offers first hand experience of positional maths language as children play. Step away from the teddy in the box, on the box and under the box, and enjoy crawling through, under, over and on top of equipment with children as they play.

Understanding the World

The key to delivering quality learning in this area is to understand that it is exactly as it says on the tin, so to speak. This area is about children making sense of the world around them from the minute they are born and using all five of their senses. I apologise if I sound a bit evangelical in this section but my teaching degree is in primary science education, and I am passionate about not turning children off science at an early age with boring, adult led 'experiments'.

Early science is about giving children an environment which screams 'come and explore me' and quickly lets them make full use of all their senses. With this in mind, lots of messy play could be viewed as science as it helps children to explore and investigate textures, materials and senses in the context of child led play. We must look at all areas of our provision, be it mud kitchen, water play, playdough or creation station and ask ourselves "are we offering multi-sensory experiences?". Early science couldn't be more far removed from the expensive, plastic resources on offer through educational suppliers. It really is about looking at the world around us and using all that is cheap and free for the taking. It's about asking "who?", "when?", "why?", "where?" and "what if?". Not a float and sink experiment in sight!

Investigation station building

In *Literacy* and in *Mathematics* I have advocated looking for learning in all areas of play around our settings. I don't hesitate to do exactly the same for *Understanding the World*, but also feel strongly that the development of an area set aside purely to provoke curiosity, inquiry and open ended questioning can only benefit children's learning in this field. Far from the traditional 'science display tables' of old, an investigation station is all about trying to create an "I can't keep my hands off" feeling. It should ideally include some elements that flow from children's interests such as exploring torches, magnets or bugs balanced with offering additional objects and resources that make the most of our ever-changing weather and season patterns. Lightboxes are great for exploring a wide range of materials but are easily made by adding LED christmas lights to an opaque, plastic storage box. You can even place objects such as lemon slices, raw eggs and tomatoes into laminating pouches and seal with an iron to create observation pouches to look at on your lightbox once you have built it.

Collections of natural materials, rocks, shells and bones can be kept to put out on a rolling cycle to keep interest and curiosity to a maximum. If you don't have the time to collect objects yourself, why not give all children a paper takeaway bag with a list of things you are looking for and ask them to go on a treasure hunt with their parents? Even the table you use can be cheaply upcycled to make it more interesting. Mine is covered with old maps, but we have also used sticky mirror paper to cover an old coffee table. Remember to think about all of the senses and add in cheap pots of growing herbs from supermarkets for extra sensory stimulation.

Upcycling

Understanding the world is not just about early science but should also embrace the children's immediate world and community and with a little bit of effort you can upcycle some early years staples to create stimulating resources to maximise the potential in this area. Try taking pictures of local landmarks and shops and gluing them to wooden building blocks to allow children to add places that they know into their imaginative play. Making 'mini me's' from plastic lids and laminated pictures of the children gives them the opportunity to place themselves and their friends into their small world play situations as they choose.

You can even upcycle an old sand or water tray to become a 'child safe' raised pond, adding water plants to help it mature and encourage wildlife to move in. Always risk assess around water and make sure you place some rocks into the water so should you get some amphibious visitors they are able to get out without drowning.

Our bug hotel is, again, just a pile of upcycled materials including pallets, straw, bricks and flower pots. It is amazing how quickly the insects will start to move in.

Old table upcycled with sticky backed mirror vinyl

reuse ... recycle ... reclaim

Donation tree

One brilliant way we have found of topping up our sensory play and investigation station is to develop a parents' donation tree in our entrance foyer. The tree has leaves which each show easy to find resources that a parent could donate at extremely low cost. Parents take the leaf off and take it home, returning with the item on the leaf as a donation. The key to success is to keep the requests cheap and easy to get hold of so that all families, irrespective of financial situations can feel they are able to contribute. Ours has saved us a fortune in items such as shaving foam, rice, spaghetti and glitter over the years leaving desperately stretched funds free for other uses.

Information Technology

Thinking about I.T. in early years we again have to look at children's lives and see what kinds of technology they come into contact with on a daily basis. Then we look to reflect that in our settings. Add in cameras, remote controls for TVs, microwaves (real if possible with cable cut off), digital and analogue clocks, digital and analogue watches, stopwatches and torches. All of these can be sourced easily at little to no cost, especially if you put a plea out to parents. Mobile phones are great for exploring the use of technology and for early communication and maths development. The next time you are in a mobile phone shop ask if they have any old 'dummy phones'. These are the ex-display phones which do not contain working parts or batteries and cannot from the company's viewpoint be recycled and resold. You can also source lots of very cheap remote control toys from car boots sales and charity shops. Certain fast food outlets have toys that often have buttons or switches that make the toys move or light up and these can be easily collected with a parent plea or a cheeky visit to said hamburger outlet.

One of our most used areas is our tinker station, as mentioned in *Physical Development*. Some of the items we have also added to it to build curiosity and investigation are light switches, magnets and solar powered light bulbs. If it has a switch or a button then it builds children's I.T. skills.

That said we can also maximise our tablets and cameras using them not only to record observations and access apps but to photograph children's small world figures as they role play to create story boards or even stop frame animation. We can access the internet (safely with supervision) to find the answers to children's questions and to watch live feed of nature. BBC Springwatch is a favourite with our children to have on the tablet at the snack table as it provokes loads of talk and excitement! You can access lots of useful free apps for use on tablets and others such as QR code generators which allow you to produce codes to place around your setting to link tablets and other learning.

We just need to remember that I.T. in early years is not all about computers!

Expressive Arts and Design

Creativity is the way in which we, as humans, express ourselves to the world. We may choose to draw, paint, sing, dance or act out a story. How we express our own creativity is a very personal thing and hence, getting all children to make a hedgehog, paint a tiger or make a Christmas card does little to tap into this individuality and nothing for children's confidence and enthusiasm for expressing their own ideas. We really do not need to create to display but we do need to display creativity.

Processes NOT Product

Children in early years need opportunities to explore a wide range of processes and not be asked to produce a defined end-product, where they will inevitably only compare their own work with that of others, instead of celebrating their achievement in exploring and problem solving along the way. Rather than waiting to the end, we need to support children as they work out how they can put their ideas into action, what materials they want to use and how to overcome problems along the way. To be able to feel that they can follow their own ideas young children need a chance to access a very wide range of open ended materials that they can explore with, manipulate and develop.

Expressive Arts and Design

reuse ... recycle ... reclaim

Creation station

Developing open ended, independent access to exciting, beautiful and inviting materials is key to EAD provision. Children need to see what they are able to use, know that they can use it whenever they wish and feel that the adults around them will support them in their pursuit of their own ideas. A creation station does not have to cost a fortune. An old book case filled with shallow baskets from a charity shop will suffice. Collect craft materials in sales and end of season lines, ask parents to donate glue sticks, glitter, pom-poms etc. Keep recycled packaging for children to use in their constructions (turning cardboard boxes inside out and re-taping gives a surface that is much more receptive to glue, paint and glitter. Try approaching supermarkets after Christmas or Easter, they may donate the craft materials, wrapping paper and ribbons etc. rather than sending them to landfill.

Expressive Arts and Design

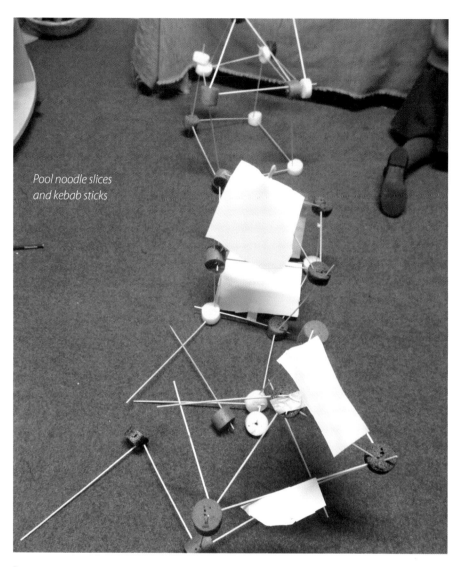

Pool noodle slices and kebab sticks

Loose parts

Creativity isn't just limited to cutting, sticking and painting. We need to make sure we have lots of loose parts in our settings which allow children to build, design and to create whenever and wherever they wish. We have to provide the power of possibility to our children and facilitate the process of creativity as it occurs. Collecting all sorts of materials from scrap stores, gardens and pound shops means this does not have to cost a fortune.

Note: Always risk assess and supervise when using small parts with young children.

Scrap stores

Your local scrap store will be a great source of cheap resources. They are usually cheap to join and a real treasure trove of recycled materials. You should be able to stock up on creative bits and bobs, as well as staples such as paper, paint and material. See the useful information section at the end of the book for where to find your local scrapstore.

Deconstructed play

When it comes to role play, as well as the need for home corner provision, at all times, so that children can revisit experiences from home, we can also provide what is known as deconstructed role play experiences. Providing a selection of boxes, fabrics, hats and other materials so that children can create what they want, be what they want and become whoever they wish. This provision is often offered as something special and different, when it should really be access to these materials at all times as part of ongoing provision alongside more structured role play areas.

Real life play

As we have discussed in other sections of the book there are great benefits to children being able to revisit familiar experiences. As well as those items identified to help build maths, literacy and a home from home feel, we can collect other 'real life' role play props cheaply, if not free. Asking charity shops to save hats rather than throw them away is a great way of getting hold of open ended resources and saving them from landfill and raiding your wardrobes and cupboards will give you other play items that have huge imaginative potential without the need for expensive specific costumes. Try collecting a briefcase, real shoes, hair brushes and bobbles. Scarves in lots of fabrics and colours can one day be a superhero cloak and the next a wedding veil. Children have amazing imaginations if we only give them the tools to tap into their own ideas.

Conclusion

And so, I hope that within these pages you have been able to find not only an outline of good, child led learning within exciting and engaging environments, but also some inspiration from the many pictures from a wide variety of settings who have successfully developed good, early years practice with little or no money. Just because we provide outstanding opportunities for our children does not mean it has to come at an enormous price. By being creative, thinking a little outside of the normal purchase routes and having the courage to ask around you too can enable your setting to deliver fantastic learning on a shoestring. Enjoy building your resource collections and opening up your settings to the power of possibility and the potential for learning.

Useful Information

Scrapstoresuk.org – a directory of scrapstores across the UK

Natural resources – great reasonably priced natural resources available from www.bakerross.co.uk

Tyres – Easily sourced from tyre fitters and garages. Smaller tyres could be sourced from go-karting tracks.

Cable reels – Try your local electrical supplier/fitter.

Recycled goods – Many recycling centres have shop outlets where you can buy items, including furniture, at a really cheap price. Ask your local centre where they send their nearly new goods.

Wood slices – Try contacting your local tree surgeon or parks department to see if you can have a donation of log slices for free or a minimal charge. If you have a Forestry Commission site near you they may be able to supply you with some logs.

Pebbles – It is illegal in the UK to remove pebbles from beaches due to the potential impact on costal erosion so make sure you use 'river washed cobbles' from DIY or garden centres.

Wooden pallets – These are easily sourced from most industrial estates. Make sure you check for nails and splinters and DO NOT use blue pallets as this have been coated with chemicals.

Charity shops – It is worth giving charity shops a list of things you are looking for as much of what they routinely throw away is early years treasure. Teapots with no lids, metal treasures, saucepans for mud kitchens etc.

Grants – When you need to find some funds don't forget to try local charitable sources. The Rotary Club, Lions Club, Round Table and even Freemasons all have pots of money for local projects. The Co-op have a community support scheme and can do anything from providing free snack fruit to donating via their member card scheme. Tesco have a community project where a proportion of the charge for bags is distributed locally.

Remember... if you don't ask, you won't get! Happy hunting.

References

Statutory framework for the early years foundation stage – Setting the standards for learning, development and care for children birth to five – DFE 2017 – London.

More information about The Curiosity Approach visit www.thecuriosityapproach.com

Conclusion